MW01128781

A MISGUIDED THOUGHT REVELATION INTO THE LIGHT

Book of Poetry

BY: JAELYN JORDAN

Djs legacy incorporated

A MISGUIDED THOUGHT REVELATION INTO THE LIGHT

Copyright © 2022 by by: Jaelyn Jordan

All rights reserved. No part of this book may be reproduced in any manner whatsoever without written permission except in the case of brief quotations embodied in critical articles and reviews.

First Printing, 2022

CONTENTS

I dedicate this book to all the lost souls in the world,
To everyone that feels lost or alone
may my words guide you and bring you solace, let me be your
inner voice be your guiding light, by grace through faith
I dedicate this book to all of our " Misguided Thoughts"!

A Misguided Thought

Vol. 2
Revelation Into The Light
By: Jaelyn D. Jordan

CHAPTER 1

Challenge Me

Challenge me
Full as the moon at its peak, my faith shines!
A passion that spawned hope within
Faith, keeping my mind open to imagine
A guiding light that I prayed for, a light I now see,
But what if this light I see, is not shining on this relic because it's
what I need but shimmering over it for that's the obstacle, the
object that challenges me. A guiding light I prayed for as full as the
moon at its peak, ready to shine to inspire to challenge me.

CHAPTER 2

Fly Free

Fly Free

Trying to strive to succeed but this life isn't for me feeling caged like a bird praying that One day I can also fly free but at what cost does freedom come to me, acting off impulse one can't understand why everything I desire intel's another woman or man, a merging of the minds is what I think I seek but again at what cost to me? Actually afraid and trembling at the thought I could lose you , over something history has showed me it's what we use to do, and yes as the words pour out my mouth I can come to say I love you, but I see within my thoughts I'm losing you, leaving me stuck, stranded in my thoughts , feeling hopeless like I don't know what to do, but with all my questions of what if I realized that nothing not even a desire is worth

losing you, so a trapped bird I must be for certain birds aren't prepared to fly away free.

CHAPTER 3

Death will take its toll

Let your true desires go unfed
&
Death will take its toll.

CHAPTER 4

Draining

Giving, giving, giving
Constantly taking away from me,
Why must I feel like taking care of you is my responsibility with
no gratitude,
yet I bleed for you,
selfish you are! I wish I could be like you,
I wish I could compete with you,
Giving so much of me what's left for me
When am I able to breathe
Sinking, drowning by the weights of my own sorrows because
my heart just wants to be fed.

CHAPTER 5

Transparent Love

It's tragic how my love tends to fade,
Leaving nothing but ever-lasting heartache in my way, so pure ,
perfect & true! yet it's sad to say I no longer want you, it's not riches
I desire that sure you can provide, it's not the protection or amor
that you can provide but the lack of adventure, the lack of knowledge of the outside world, the view of the world alone is knowledge,
knowledge not given by men but by faith and it's this adventure
you wish not to let me partake .
No matter how perfect or how much love, nothing compares to
a thrill seekers love.

CHAPTER 6

Poetry Man

From my lips wisdom spews.
From my heart comes compassion and faith.
From my touch comes gold and my presence peace, not because
I think highly of myself or because folks I know pat me on the back
but because when I come to speak, I speak of words of healing and
light, when I use and open my heart , I clear out the darkness and
the pain , and when I come to use my hands , I'm helping build a
new life for us all , for we all running and seeking something,
seeking strength!
Seeking the true purpose of life, through my words by grace
through faith I'll be your guiding light.

CHAPTER 7

Influencing me

Sometimes I just want to break down and cry
I just want to give up, I've been trying my best to control my
thoughts but I need Help Lord.
Someone please help me, I know it's no one's responsibility but
mine but I can't do it alone for I am too far gone . I'm trying to
escape this mental prison but my demons won't let me .They make
sure I drown in the misery I created for myself blocking me from
Gods blessings , not allowing me to be my best self, clouding my
mind with negative thoughts and false perceptions, getting my
hopes up just to steal every bit of happiness that's comes my way as
if it's some sort of joke . How can I keep laughing at my pain when
the pain keeps getting worse? I don't know how long I can keep
walking around with a smile so I ask from the heavens above to fill
my heart with love and my mind with peace
for the worlds pain is negatively influencing me.

CHAPTER 8

Emptiness Inside

What's this new emptiness I feel inside?
An unfulfilled feeling, yanking and dragging me by chains
through the street for all my suffering to lay bare as if my pain
stands for a good comedy show to the world, what am I seeking?
Peace? Love? Happiness? No, I'm seeking to feel anything again, to
feel any emotion, for my soul is black, no life inside, just lost souls
trying to survive, how can I feed this emptiness inside? Nothing,
not even my faith makes me feel alive. I feel so dead inside.

CHAPTER 9

Everlasting fog

Lost in an ever-lasting fog of smoke
it's all a mask
Smiling for the cameras like my pain has faded
Trying to achieve the ultimate dream, but at what cost to me,
pushing through the back pain and aching feet just to be able to eat,
this life isn't for me.

but I promised to share my word my message with the world to
free myself from this pain but even that comes at a cost. Do you
ever wonder why me? Well I'm sick of pondering what a happy life
would be like, it's been written for me, I want to enjoy love, bliss, I
want to enjoy gods Ultimate riches , can't you see life on earth was
the breaking point, a guide to for me to be able to deliver a message
that the material things on earth we're formed just to gnaw at your
soul , a distraction to blind you from one's purpose.

CHAPTER 10

Own you

Build the world around you, and let everyone embrace you!

CHAPTER 11

Growing

What signifies growth? Constantly telling yourself you're changing maybe. Maybe it's not acting on impulse? What if growth was simply not changing but to stop. When you think of growing as an individual, you think of changing what's bad about yourself to become what you think, is this better person, but what happens if changing the negative about yourself to grow leads you down a path of forgetting who you are in general? What then?

So now I ask what signifies growth, what signifies growth within the mind, the body, and spirit, what's the anchor between light and dark.

The answer is Love.

CHAPTER 12

True love

Joy a feeling I lost but found,
A love that grows from the bottom of my spine,
Treatment and care like in early times,
A love that's true,
A love that's free,
A love that makes songs about loving me,
A love that relit the match of passion and opened my heart.
So many bad seeds before you and boy was I blind to who I
thought i loved or what love was, but I see now!
It's the smile I see, when I close my eyes.
The missing and longing of your touch.
The sound of your breath and heart beating, your what I was
missing! This is what I'm missing!
A love that I never really knew or seen until this love seen me.

CHAPTER 13

Unnecessary war

A faceless person that lyes beneath me feet
Fighting for the right to live and breathe,
As I've witnessed and watched my whole family bleed, screams
of children cry in the smoke
Gunshot wounds I'm grateful that it didn't Pierce my throat,
my god what is this? A soldier of the night that's fighting a battle
that's not mine, while my family is stuck in a country we don't even
belong, banned by one from leaving and attacked by another for
breathing, is my life no more than another? A man of not your
country must serve but a woman of mine can't leave, in any country
we're not free, and this fight! This war this taking a toll on my body
and mind, I pray God seeps into my nightmares in the president's
dreams so that he lives with my constant agony.

CHAPTER 14

Consuming Thoughts

As time passes my mind still loops itself to play out my greatest fears , to drown myself in all despair, one would think after all the writing I did about depression and mental illness, life dealing with it would be simple or become easier as time moves on but it becomes harder, your dark thoughts consumes you and the simple pleasures you use to get out of life just seem meaning-less. All you want to do is drown, suffocate, die but to die would mean suicide. Which I would see as an option if so many people wouldn't call me selfish after or condemn me to hell, but then again to me I'm in hell trapped and enclosed by one's mind stuck trying to break free , screaming, screaming, screaming but no one to help me . One would think prayers to clear my mind and to heal me would work but what if the answer to my prayers really lied beneath me . On the edge of the cliff and I was just too afraid to jump and to afraid to share these thoughts because the only thing worse than death is being locked up. Being called mad is what they'll say or I'll get you help but the help I need is not offered here, for its the depression and fight within my mind that consumes me every day and every day even with my smile it wins.

CHAPTER 15

Grateful

Words can't express how grateful I am for you, in more ways
than one I found solace and comfort within the love you gave to
me.
Your compassionate, humble, honest, and true to yourself something beyond admiration.
I couldn't have asked for a better version of an angel in plain
sight than you.
I'm excited for this journey with you, and overjoyed to the point
where I swear I could die of happiness at this very second a little
dramatic I know, but still brings me to say your everything to me
sexy and that -
I Love You!

CHAPTER 16

Unconditional

Never in a million years would I have ever come to imagine me actually finding love , better yet being loved! Unconditionally years I've tried to mask who I was and blend in with others to be liked, or get the attention and recognition I deserved , I spent my entire childhood and up to most recently my entire adult life, taking care of others and putting my own needs lasts mentally and emotionally thinking that no matter how I felt now my pain would go away. If I could give them something they've never had, better yet if I could give my mom apart of her past she's lost by enabling her bad habits maybe that would be peace enough? I was lost, I lost sight of who I wanted to be , better yet I had lost sight of the man I've dreamt of becoming until I met you. You seen me for wat I was just an open-hearted man with a vision, you didn't see me as a piggy bank or an emotional punching bag you've seen me for what felt like the first time in forever, I felt real warmth in my heart, I felt Genuine unconditional love. I know sometimes I can be very prideful and feel like I can do everything on my own but I'm grateful that you're willing to take this journey with me and granted we might know all of each other's flaws and sometimes they will collide but you're the love of my life and no matter wat u may think I wouldn't trade you in for the world. I know you're going to hate that when we argue I smile in your face hell, I know that'll set you off and we haven't gotten there yet lol but honestly, I'm sorry but if you seen wat I see u would smile too. I see a caring compassionate individual with a badass smile and sexy ass lips why else u think I always try to kiss u mid-sentence , I see a career driven young guy that also struggles w his own but constantly putting others needs before his own most importantly wen I look at u I see my future , I see my husband and no matter what you go through and how much pain and trouble you're in I'll be right by your side helping you clean up the mess for as you chose to take this journey with me I've chosen to take the same journey with you ,I love you mi amor forever and always .

CHAPTER 17

Proud and True

A love that is profound and true
A love that fills you,
A love that both fills you and empties you
Something within your soul bonding you
To something that's so profound so true
Something real, something everlasting
Something that holds strong despite the times passing
To see past flaws and look past pain
To truly love despite all the neglect
To care despite all the carelessness
To tell the truth despite all the lies
A bright light that beams through the darkness
A warm flame that protects and comforts its inhabitants
A warmth that brings health
A health that brings security
To the thoughts that claim and fuel off disease
A love that is proud and true
A love that is you.

CHAPTER 18

A poem for you

I could spend a while talking about what the sight of you does
to me, but I won't
Or spend hours talking about how something as simple as
watching how the chains lie on your chest excites me but I can't
Or how inevitably I find you more attractive each day.
Infatuation? Maybe.
But why does it feel like you're a part of me?
But why do I consider someone's feelings whom I never felt like
considered my own?
Why can't I just let go?
If it was truly just infatuation why would these questions cross
my mind?
Truth
I ponder what our lives would be like in the future
When I daydream, I picture it
Then I slip into a dark space

Most would be in pain watching the person they're in love with give that love, attention, and affection away while they no longer get to feel it and must sit back and watch and simply be okay.
Deep down inside I await the day when I wake up and realize that I don't want you anymore, but I fear that day will not come
But our present doesn't align with the future I envision
& while I see myself legally bound to you with children in the future
My integrity, pride, and face cannot touch the floor
Because I refuse to pick them up because you made me drop them.

CHAPTER 19

lost

I've given up I keep finding myself struggling in sin I no longer can breathe, so much pain I'm numb what will make me happy? What will free my thoughts? I'm struggling, I can't breathe Is it my fault? God help me.

CHAPTER 20

The Devil in Disguise

Don't tempt me, I'm the devil in disguise.

As tyrants fall among their ashes I rise.

A stable mind that fades away, that when provoked leaves bodies in his wake,

Tread lightly when I'm near and see my smile as fake, for when u look in my eyes it's the souls I come to crave. Don't tempt me for I am the devil in disguise, seduced and drawn by my words to your grave will be your fate, manipulation is key to maintain this world, and death is key to start anew, for human life to me is nothing more than a petting zoo. Don't acknowledge me, hate me! for it makes me strong, belittle me or cry for those are key notes, words to my favorite song.

Don't see me as your savior for you will be wrong, for I am nothing less but the devil in disguise.

CHAPTER 21

A Better Me

I choose to be free! No more chasing after a dream or image of what could make me happy.

I choose to be free, to embrace love and light.

Removing all the toxic traits within myself that I'm aware of, embracing change, not letting my past hinder my future. I choose not to settle because I'm sick of being hurt, but to push through the darkness that weighs heavy in my mind and heart. I choose to be better, to be someone worth remembering, someone worth loving.

CHAPTER 22

Use It Before You Lose It

Past the trauma looking back in time, tell me how do you know you haven't just given up on what god has created and gifted to you? What if? questions arise, when alone pondering in the dark, but then you think about what triggered the list of challenges you faced, the challenges you overcame and then I ask again, past the trauma looking back in time. Tell me, how do you know you haven't just given up on what god created and gifted you?

CHAPTER 23

Buried Burdens

I consume my fears to relish in the light, drown my sorrows so
I'll be free to fly.

CHAPTER 24

A New You

Within a triggering a moment
I now see, our joint pain that had stained both our pasts, our
self-growth and self-realization coming from relationships we
thought we couldn't move past. I prayed for someone to complete
me, I prayed for someone to perfect me, and I've got you. My time
with you has filled my heart, my time with has filled my soul, your
smile is my bliss. I know your heartaches as mine does, but I have
you now, let me pick up the pieces of your heart off the floor, let me
recapture the memories of pure happiness, let you see yourself from
my point of view as I will forever come to see and understand all of
you.

CHAPTER 25

A Dream Come True

Just wanting to be looked at with pure love in your eyes, day-dreaming about those pearly white teeth, craving the echoing sound of your voice off my walls and the warm sensation of your touch. To feel my body, get hot when your near, to feel your breath on my neck, just to melt my heart,
What a dream come true.

CHAPTER 26

Self-Destruction

I set my self on a path to discover the true me, To embrace love and my future through the eyes and dreams that lye deep within my mind, but time and time again, every time I get close to what I seek I tend to lose it and inevitably end up back where I started. I've come to accept I am who I am, in more ways than one but is it because I am who I am I can't ever find the one, or is it just that when I get so close my personal insecurities , my past trauma makes me push you away? Can you open my heart to trust? To the true definition of love?

Or

Is it self-destruction?

CHAPTER 27

Denial

Denial, a six-letter word that causes me stress, a word that makes me feel inadequate to be with you. A word that backs me in the corner of my sorrows and makes me bring out my partner's ego and pride to fight the good fight for me. Denial is a word that hurts me, and although you might not be denying all of me, only that flaw or two that you see, my mind and heart only sees and hears that you don't want me. Denial is a word that'll have me end up alone, because of that word off the tongue of your mouth, no matter if you weren't going to leave me, I'm telling you I'm done.

CHAPTER 28

A Tireless Journey

I find myself on a tireless journey, stranded and alone. Seeking profound qualities within me to make me whole, seeking self-control.

Constantly falling short of one's mission detracted by the objects in the road, laying over bodies when one's feet gets tired instead of laying over hands. A tireless journey I keep myself on, with low ambition, I find myself holding out my hands for someone to pick me up so I no longer must hike this hike, a lack of self-control is what keeps me down, a lack of ambition is what keeps me unmotivated but with laying of hands and not over bodies is what will get me through this journey.

CHAPTER 29

One Last Dance

How do I know if the love is real? Is it the way I feel when you kiss me? Is it the way I smile when you tell me you miss me? How do I know it's forever? When it rains you give me shelter, when I'm at my worst you make me better. How do I know you care? When you see me down you rub your fingers through my hair but how could you love me when it's hard to love myself? When I look at you, I see perfection, but I need help. I've been broken by this world and the people in it with you I see a second chance with you I'll have one last dance.

CHAPTER 30

Love or Lust

Why does love feel so good and hurt so much at the same time I
saw the best in you and became blind. How do I live with myself
knowing I'll never be enough is it love or is it lust?

CHAPTER 31

Mixed Personalities

The smartest minds have 2 faces
How the waters move free, how I envy nothing with no moving
life force, it's the freedom I hope to have, the freedom to help is
what will Set me free,
gliding through the trees, trying to fly like the birds but I don't
move far,
my purpose is unheard, my fears my doubts keep me weak but
then when I'm triggered you don't want to meet me,
that's that smile you love so much,
it's the charm that draws you to me but this face wears horns,
when he's mad, he grows horns,
Water becomes fire and wine becomes blood but to build an
empire only one face can survive. What happened if the face that
wore horns was loved as much as mine, would that reflection of me
be nicer? What happened if I was as nice and happy as my other
face, would I be just as happy? Or would I be even teased more for
having a soft tone voice that much define my sexuality, my soft tone
that deceives all man , to fill like the world should burn in flames for

my pain, makes me wrong ,makes me a tyrant but where's my
defender where's my help , my salvation is in my hands it's the face
that's smarter than two minds.

I hate, I hate the gap of knowledge this generation limits us too,
I hate, the fact that our females forget the importance of hygiene
then expect us brothers to take care of them, or how our men treat
our females when they're pregnant or after their bare our children, I
hate, how I keep seeing brothers abuse their spouses instead of
moving on or talking things out, I hate it!
I'm scared by the world I come to cherish so, shocked and
baffled by the pain I see in everyone's eyes, searching for love,
longing, a place in life, searching for peace amongst chaos and darkness, so many negatives in this world, it becomes easy to form the
word hate, that deprives itself from the true words love! A movement, a touch, a spark of hope,
a movement, a touch, a spark of love
A movement, a touch, words of faith
is all it takes!
friends, family, a village, is what will remove all the hate.

Good Day,
My name Is Jaelyn D. Jordan and Thank you so much for supporting
me in my fight in highlighting mental health awareness, for those of you
that may not know I am a registered behavioral therapist that has set his
hopes and desires on combing what I love to do most in this life with gods
purpose for me! I truly believe that's helping everyone on earth understand
their thoughts, hopes, dreams desires and to cure ones fears so at the age of
24 I've decided to truly walk by faith through grace and use words of
poetry and my own experiences suffering from manic depression, lack of
stability and support and turn it into treasured gold for all.
by grace through faith, in a world filled with darkness , My only desire is
to be that beam of light for everyone.

**A Misguided
Thought QR Code**

CPSIA information can be obtained
at www.ICGtesting.com
Printed in the USA
LVHW082048260223
740083LV00002B/1